Portrait of the Past
THE CIVIL WAR ON ROANOKE ISLAND
NORTH CAROLINA

—A Pictorial Tour—

To: Terry —
Thanks for your
interest in the Civil War
on the Outer Banks.

Drew Pullen

10/3/2002

Officers of the *USS Wabash*

The publication of this book would not have been possible without the generosity of the following sources:

We would like to thank The Casemate Museum in Fort Monroe, VA; National Archives Special Media Division, still pictures, College Park, MD;

Brian Edwards, Sarah Downing and the Outer Banks History Center at the North Carolina Division of Archives and History in Manteo, NC; Currier and Ives; El-Co Color Lab in Manalapan, NJ;

the Champney family of Bedford, MA; our editor, Torrey Kim, congratulations on the new addition to your family; graphic designer Kathy Zaremba; manufacturing agent Laura Livingston, Max

Graphics; Beverly R. Robinson Collection, United States Naval Academy Museum, Annapolis, MD; North Carolina Department of Cultural Resources/Underwater Archaeology Branch,

Kure Beach, NC; Museum of the Albemarle in Elizabeth City, NC; United States Naval Historical Center, Washington, DC; North Carolina Collection,

University of North Carolina Library at Chapel Hill; Fort Branch, NC; Northeastern Historic Places Office Division of Archives and History; Charles T. Skinner; Mike Tames;

Alex H. Leary, Gun Collection and Assistant; Captain Albert Jarvis and Captain Woody Spencer, surgeons; Phillip Jenkins and Roger Williams, Confederate Re-enactors, NC; "Hubby" Bliven;

The renactment hosted by Camp Olden Civil War Round Table & Museum and the Township of Hamilton, NJ; Scotty Sword; Kathleen Myers a.k.a. Mom, artist and illustrator;

and our wives, Christy Drapala and Jo Anne Pullen, for their support, patience, and love.

From the staff of Aerial Perspective our thoughts and prayers are with our men and women who serve our country. Our deepest sympathies to the families who lost loved ones on September 11, 2001.

Published by Aerial Perspective / Robert V. Drapala Publishing / 428 Cripps Drive / Mt. Holly / New Jersey 08060 / www.aerialperspective.com

ISBN 0-9660586-6-6

Printed in China

Portrait of the Past
THE CIVIL WAR ON ROANOKE ISLAND
NORTH CAROLINA
—A Pictorial Tour—

Written by Drew Pullen
Photographs by Robert V. Drapala
Design by Katherine P. Zaremba

The Civil War on Roanoke Island North Carolina

Roanoke Island, like Hatteras Island, is rich in history. Union soldiers involved in the attack

on Roanoke Island were aware that the first attempt at English colonization in the New World occurred on the island they were occupying.

In fact, the land and shores of the Outer Banks were directly touched by the earliest period of exploration (Verrazzano), colonization (Lost Colony), the American Revolution and War of 1812 (English attacked houses and villages on the Outer Banks), the Civil War, and World Wars I and II (German U-boats sank allied ships on the coast).

The Civil War came to Roanoke Island after Hatteras Island fell under Federal control in August of 1861. Once the Union controlled Hatteras Inlet, the door was opened to take control of all of North Carolina's inland waters, except the area near

Edwin Graves Champney

left: Aerial view of Roanoke Island

Bombardment of the Forts of Hatters Island Inlet, North Carolina, circa 1861

the 31st North Carolina troops. The 46th and 48th Virginia were also assigned to defend the island.

Although most of the attention to Roanoke Island's history has focused on Sir Walter Raleigh's "Lost Colony," an increasing interest is being directed at the Civil War action that occurred there. A Civil War Trail was recently established, at which monuments were placed on Roanoke Island, Hatteras Island, and Ocracoke to commemorate the battles fought on the Outer Banks.

All of the drawings featured in this book are from the Civil War period. Personal letters and quotes from soldiers allow the reader to get a feel for what life was like during the War in North Carolina. Many of the letters included in this book were written by Captain William Chace of the 4th Rhode Island, which was among the troops selected for Brigadier General Ambrose Burnside's well-known expedition.

The regiment arrived in Annapolis, Maryland, on the 8th of January, 1862, and prepared to embark on the steamer *Eastern Queen*, their destination still unknown. In Chace's letters to his father (who held the rank of Major), he describes in great detail the movements of the regiment, along with accounts of soldier life in general. Included are personal touches, such as when Chace directs his father to handle his pay, which he encloses in his letters.

Chace and the 4th Rhode Island survived the storms of Hatteras and the battle of Roanoke Island with no casualties.

Fort Fisher in Wilmington. A small group of Confederate soldiers of the 7th North Carolina troops escaped from Hatteras during the Federal assault, and fled to Roanoke Island, where they joined with members of the 3rd Georgia to prepare for Roanoke Island's defense. In December of 1861, the 3rd Georgia was removed and replaced with

Unfortunately, they wouldn't be as lucky in the next campaign.

Also included in the book are soldiers' drawings and sketches by Edwin Graves Champney and his cousin James Wells Champney. J.W. Champney was a soldier stationed at Fort Macon, North Carolina

An actual letter to Captain Chace's father, Major John R. Chace.

Captain William Chace

during the Civil War. Although he did not visit the Outer Banks during the War, his drawings are included to offer readers an idea of what life was like during that period in North Carolina. In addition, the book features clips from newspapers such as *Harper's Weekly*, *Frank Leslie's Illustrated Newspaper*, and *Currier and Ives*, whose artists illustrated scenes of battles and the soldiers' lives through pencil sketches, pen and ink drawings, and paintings. These vintage illustrations, combined with new photography, that visually depicts what the soldiers saw and experienced, create a stunning visual experience of the campaign.

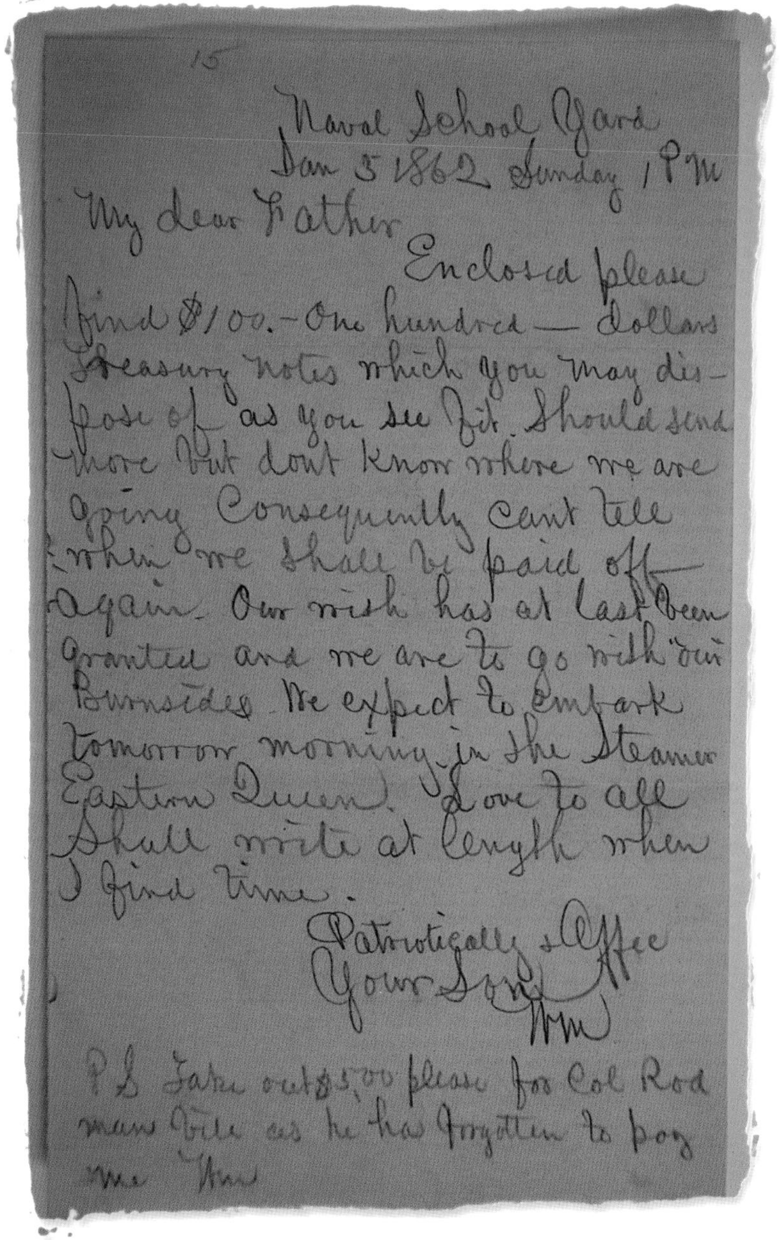

15

Naval School Yard
Jan 5 1862 Sunday, 1 P.M.
My dear Father
Enclosed please find $100.– One hundred — dollars Treasury notes which you may dispose of as you see fit. Should send more but dont know where we are going Consequently cant tell when we shall be paid off again. Our wish has at last been granted and we are to go with "our" Burnsides. We expect to embark tomorrow morning in the Steamer Eastern Queen. Love to all Shall write at length when I find time.
Patriotically & Affec
Your Son
Wm

P.S. Take out $5.00 please for Col Rodman as he has forgotten to pay me Wm

Naval School Yard
Jan 5 1862 Sunday 1 PM

My dear Father

Enclosed please find $100 - One hundred - dollars Treasury notes which you may dispose of as you see fit. Should send more but don't know where we are going consequently cant tell when we shall be paid off again. Our wish has at last been granted and we are to go with "our" Burnsides. We expect to embark tomorrow morning in the Steamer Eastern Queen. Love to all shall write at length when I find time.

Patriotically + Affec
Your Son
Wm

PS Take out $5.00 please for Col Rodman as he has forgotten to pay me Wm

James Wells Champney

James Wells Champney was a soldier stationed at Fort Macon, North Carolina during the Civil War. Although he did not visit Roanoke Island during the War, his drawings of his fellow soldiers offer a unique perspective of life during the Civil War along the coastal waters of North Carolina. The soldier featured in this picture is relaxing and writing home, much like William Chace would have done.

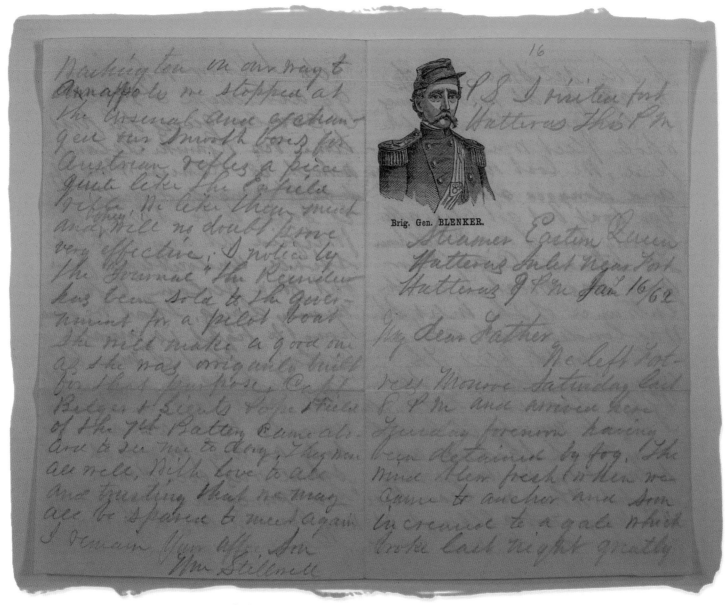

Brig. Gen. BLENKER.

Actual letters of Captain William Chace, from the collection of Mike Tames.

Steamer Eastern Queen
Hatteras Inlet near Fort Hatteras PM Jan 16/62

My dear Father

We left Fort Monroe Saturday last 8 PM and arrived here Sunday forenoon having been detained by fog. The wind blew fresh when we came to anchor and soon increased to a gale which broke last night greatly to the satisfaction of us all for at many times it looked as though the whole fleet would be wrecked. We lost our bowes and dragged afoul of a gunboat but got clear after losing part of our wheel house. The steamer City of New York was wrecked at the entrance of the inlet. She was loaded with ordnance stores for the fleet. The Commodore thinks the pilot did it intentionally. I think myself it looks very much that way as he went on in broad daylight. When we leave here I know not, although it must be quite soon neither do I know where we go although I think I could guess the first time is Roanoke Island which is between Pamlico & Albemarle Sounds. It is said to be strongly fortified at any rate we shall undoubtedly find out for certain before many days. That we shall have to fight is morally certain that I may do my duty is my prayer if I do and fall in so doing remember tis in a cause as holy as any for which a sword was ever drawn.

Rifles left to right: Springfield, 1864; Enfield, 1853; 1809 Prussian Musket; Austrian Lorenz, 1861; Enfield Carbine "Barnet;" Henry Rifle; Ballard Carbine; Union Calvary Sword

"God moves in a mysterious way his wonders to perform." As we passed through Washington on our way to Annapolis we stopped at the arsenal and exchanged our smooth bores for Austrian rifles, a piece quite like the Enfield rifle. We like them much and they will do no doubt prove very effective. I notice by the "journal" the Reindeer has been sold to the government for a pilot boat. She will make a good one as she was originally built for that purpose. Capt Belger & Lieuts Pope & Field of the 7th Battery came aboard to see me today. They were all well. With love to all and trusting that we may all be spared to meet again I remain Your Affec. Son

Wm Stillwell

P.S. I visited Fort Hatteras this PM

Burnside's Expedition at Hatteras

On January 12, 1862, Brigadier General Ambrose E. Burnside's expedition left the security of Fort Monroe in Hampton, Virginia, and sailed south under the command of Flag Officer Louis Malesherbes Goldsborough. Their aim was to gain control of North Carolina's inland waters and threaten the Confederate supply lines.

Brigadier General Ambrose E. Burnside and Flag Officer L.M. Goldsborough

NAVAL BATTLE OF ROANOKE ISLAND

During late January, 1862, a Federal land-sea expedition assembled at Hatteras Inlet to take Roanoke Island and capture control of the North Carolina Sound - region. This force was under the joint command of General Ambrose Burnside and navy Flag-Officer Louis Goldsborough. After several delays due to bad weather, the Union fleet, consisting of numerous troop transports and more than 20 war vessels, arrived at the southern end of Roanoke Island. On February 7, 1862, Federal warships (O) bombarded Fort Bartow (J), southernmost of the Confederate defenses.

The fort returned the fire but with little effect. The Confederate fleet (N), under Captain W.F. Lynch, waited to engage the Federals behind a line of obstructions (M) placed in Croatan Sound to retard the Federal advance.

However, the Confederate fleet, after a sharp engagement which was ended only by darkness, was forced to retire due to a lack of ammunition. On February 8, 1862, the Federal fleet bombarded various positions on Roanoke Island in support of General Burnside's land offensive. After the Union victory on the afternoon of February 8, a detachment of Federal ships under Commander S. C. Rowan was sent into Albemarle Sound in pursuit of the Confederate fleet. The Union forces were now in control of most of the inland waters of northeastern North Carolina.

Civil War Trail marker

"We left Fort Monroe Saturday last 8 PM and arrived here Sunday forenoon having been detained by fog."
  - WM Chace

Sketch of Fort Monroe, circa 1860

Aerial view of Fort Monroe

PORTRAIT OF THE PAST
11
THE CIVIL WAR ON ROANOKE ISLAND

Sketch of a balloon aerial of Fort Monroe

Aerial view of Fort Monroe

After surviving weeks of severe winter storms off of Hatteras, the expedition, consisting of more than 12,000 men on 60 ships, passed through Hatteras Inlet and made some much needed repairs.

Not every ship completed its mission: those lost in the storms included the *City of New York*, a steam transport carrying supplies, and the Army gunboat *Zouaves*. Life aboard the transport ships during these two major storms was extremely trying. Colonel Thomas Edmands of the 24th Massachusetts described his experiences:

> *Life on the transports was weariness and vexation… Measles broke out on some of the vessels whose crowded condition defied proper sanitary precautions, and many poor fellows were carried to shallow graves scooped in the sands near (Hatteras Inlet).*[1]

Union vessel

Hatteras Lighthouse, 1863   Edwin Graves Champney

"...for at many times it looked as though the whole fleet would be wrecked."

Hatteras storm off the coast of Frisco, North Carolina.

"Just then the splendid and commodious steamer City of New York attempted to run in, but the rough sea, handling her as if she was a mere egg-shell...

The wreck of the *City of New York* off the coast of Hatteras, January 13, 1862.

...threw her upon the beach, and in less than 20 minutes that mammoth steamer was lashed to pieces by the angry breakers."

History of the 51st Regiment of Pennsylvania Volunteers

next page: Wreckage of the *City of New York* along Hatteras Beach.

Hatteras storm

Not only did these troops suffer from measles, but the barges carrying barrels of water supplies for the expedition were lost at sea. In addition, several of the ships collided with one another as they dragged anchor in the storms, and had to be repaired when they reached the quiet shelter of Pamlico Sound.

Lifeboats

Life saving station at Cape Hatteras

Steamer Eastern Queen
Wednesday Jan 22 1862

My Dear Father

    Am blessed with good health and
hope I may be allowed to return to you all if not we
shall all meet hereafter. Cannot write more at length

      Affec + Patriotically
      Your Son Wm

Edwin Graves Champney

Wreck of the *Zouave*

"The Army gunboat Zouave, with a number of 23rd men detailed on her, overrun her anchor, knocked a hole in her bottom, and sank where her upper deck was just awash."

Record of the 23rd Massachusetts Volunteer Infantry

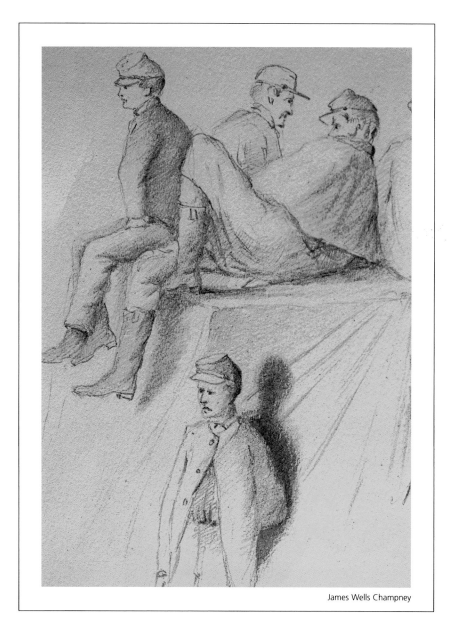

James Wells Champney

Edwin Graves Champney

After much repair and rest, at least 12,000 men were ready to depart Hatteras Inlet with the sole intention of gaining control of North Carolina's inland waters, including Roanoke Island.

left: Following the winter storms off the coast of Hatteras Island, North Carolina, the soldiers had to wait for the completion of the ship repairs. This is what it may have looked like while the soldiers relaxed prior to departing for Roanoke Island.

Boat Building

Hatteras Inlet   Edwin Graves Champney

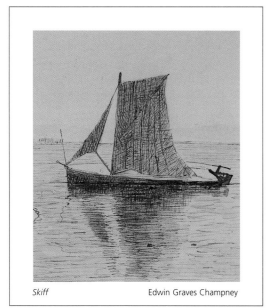

Skiff   Edwin Graves Champney

Pamlico Sound Jan 31/62
4th Regt R I Volunteers
Park's Brigade
Burnside's Division

My dear Sister Harriett
    ...I notice the Journal of the 17th which, I think, feels confident that
Burnside's Expedition was not bound south of Hatteras. The build of the vessels
in his fleet would not admit of any such proceeding, but if I can believe my
"eyes" we are south of Hatteras, and I think I have had evidence enough to
convince any sane person of that fact....
    ...I think we shall leave here my Monday next and if we are successful,
which I feel confident we shall be. Next April will see this rebellion
virtually ended.....

Sailing to Roanoke Island

On the morning of February 5, 1862, the *Delaware* gave the signal for every one of the more than 60 ships in the expedition to set off from Hatteras. Private D.L. Day of the 25th Massachusetts described that morning:

The clink of the windlass is heard on all the boats hoisting up their anchors, so here we go for a trip up the sound, probably for Roanoke Island…Our fleet consists of about 70 sails of all kinds and makes an imposing appearance. The gunboats, under the command of Commodore Goldsborough, take the advance, the transports and other craft following.[2]

General Burnside's Expedition

…I will inquire about the young man in Co F. Mary's friend in the New Hampshire Regt I saw 2 or 3 times, I forgot if I mentioned it previously. I liked his appearance much.

The weather here is quite warm, an overcoat being at most times uncomfortable….

None of the boys, with the exception of Wheaton White Balch and Manton, have written me. If they know the pleasure letters from the would give me, I think they would be willing to sacrifice a few moments of their leisure hours and they must be as plenty as gales at Hatteras inlet in doing. With love to Father, Mother, Brothers, Sisters and friends and hoping that I may be spared to return to you all sound in body + mind and reputation untarnished.

I remain your affec
Brother William

N.B. I scarce ever receive any papers from the family.
Letters come prompt enough

By late afternoon of February 5th, the fleet was within 10 miles of Roanoke Island. One of the ships continued its course toward the island to explore while the other vessels dropped anchor for the night near the town of Stumpy Point.

Flag Officer L.M. Goldsborough

Aerial of Pamlico Sound in the evening

Burnside's Expedition, steam-wheeler *Spalding*

Several of the ships comprising Burnside's fleet were shallow draft steam-wheelers, designed for rivers or the Chesapeake Bay. One of these, the *Union*, was used to transport troops. Conditions on the *Union* were extremely crowded that night and were exceedingly uncomfortable. Charles F. Johnson, a member of the 9th New York, *Hawkins Zouaves*, described the following conditions:

> *Our quarters were on the first gun-deck, our Company on the left and E on the right, but in such a small place that it was necessary to sleep packed in a somewhat fishy fashion, head and feet alternating, and when thus arranged, we covered the deck so completely that it was impossible to go either forward or aft, without treading on a very carpet of men.*[3]

James Wells Champney

Crowded quarters aboard ship—Pamilico Sound.

Roanoke Island Marsh Lighthouse

Captain Parker of the CSN was a naval officer on board the *Beaufort*, a ship of the *Mosquito Fleet*. He described his activities that evening:

> At sunset, as we saw no disposition on the part of the enemy to move, we anchored and all hands went to supper. We kept guard boats out during the night to avoid a surprise. After getting something to eat I went on board Seabird to see Commodore Lynch. I found him in his dressing gown sitting quietly in his cabin reading Ivanhoe…We talked for a long time of what the next day would probably bring…neither of us believed that we would be successful, nor was there a naval officer in the squadron who thought we would.[4]

That same night, the Confederates on Roanoke Island were aware of the Federal fleet and were attempting to prepare for action and defense as best they could.

The Federal expedition awakened the morning of February 7th to find the fleet covered in a thick fog. By nine that morning, the fog had lifted and the *Delaware* again signaled for the fleet to get underway. As the ships approached Croatan Sound on the west side of the island, all of the fortifications came into view. The fleet immediately moved toward Fort Bartow, located at Pork Point.

Top to bottom, left to right: John A. Winslow, L.M. Goldsborough, Sam J. Dupont, John A. Bahlgran, and S.H. Stringham

Sunset on Croatan Sound

"The fleet consisted of some 30 gunboats, 9 or 10 steamers with troops on board, and numerous sailing vessels, perhaps 60 to 75 all told....

Fleet passing through marshes between Croatan and Pamlico Sound.

...The fleet moved slowly along and certainly a more magnificent sight was never before seen on this side of the Atlantic."

The 25th Massachusetts Volunteers

Aerial view of the approximate location of Fort Bartow, Roanoke Island.

The Federal Assault on Roanoke Island

*A*s a light sprinkling of rain began, the Federal gunboats opened fire on Fort Bartow at 11:23 a.m. on February 7th. The Confederate *Mosquito Fleet* attempted to draw the Union ships into a series of obstructions in Croatan Sound, but the Union sailors avoided the obstacles, and instead returned fire, damaging the *Forrest* and the *Curlew*. Union vessels began landing their troops near a location called Ashby's Landing at about 4:00 in the afternoon. General Burnside described the landing of his troops as follows:

> Orders were given for the troops to land.
> The ground in the rear of Ashby's Harbor
> was cleared [of enemy troops] by shells from
> the naval vessels, and our large surf-boats
> were lowered [from the troopships], rapidly
> filled with troops, and towed in long lines by

[steamships]…until they came near to the shore of the harbor, when each of the surf-boats was cut loose and steered for the shore…In less than an hour 4,000 troops were ashore.[5]

USS Spalding

Brigadier General Ambrose E. Burnside

Brigadier General Ambrose E. Burnside and staff—"Before"

Major General Ambrose E. Burnside (promoted March 18, 1862) and staff—"After"

EARLY COAST OPERATIONS IN NORTH CAROLINA.

left: Early coast operations of Roanoke Island, North Carolina

Aerial view of Roanoke Island (1) Ashby's Harbor; (2) Fort Bartow (3) Pork Point (4) Fort Blanchard; (5) Fort Huger (6) Fort Defiance (three-gun earthworks)

"At 9am we observed the enemy to be underweigh and coming up, and we formed 'line abreast' in the rear of the obstructions...."

Bombardment of Fort Bartow, Roanoke Island

...At 11:30 the fight commenced at long range. The enemy's fire was aimed at Fort Bartow and our vessels, and we soon became warmly engaged."

Recollections of a Naval Officer by William H. Parker

"At about 11:30am on the 7th of February, the ball was opened by a shot from one of our vessels...

...and the bombardment became general as the vessels could get into position."

William L. Welch

The Burnside Expedition, and the engagement at Roanoke Island

23rd Massachusetts Infantry

USS Spalding

THE CIVIL WAR ON ROANOKE ISLAND

Troops landing on Roanoke Island

Marshes in the Roanoke Island landing area

The troops struggled ashore from their landing craft as the area consisted of swamp, marsh, bog, and a thick growth of brush including thorns. One of Burnside's men said, "My company landed after dark, on, it seemed to me, a quaking bog. I had hardly started from the boats, making for a fire on shore when my right leg went into a bog hole up to my hips."[6]

Roanoke Island Marsh Lighthouse, Kathleen C. Myers

Present-day photograph of the area where troops first landed on Roanoke Island.

Attack on Roanoke Island by Commodore Goldsborough's gunboats.

While the landing of the Federal troops was going well, the Confederate troops in Forts Blanchard, Huger, and Bartow were receiving an intense bombardment from the Union naval vessels. A Confederate naval officer on board the *Beaufort* described the bombardment this way:

> *The enemy's fire was aimed at Fort Bartow and our vessels, and we soon became warmly engaged...At 2 p.m. the firing was hot and heavy, and continued so until sunset. Our gunners had no practice with their rifled guns, and our firing was not what it should have been.*[7]

The area where the troops of General Forster, Reno, and Parks first landed on Roanoke Island.

THE CIVIL WAR ON ROANOKE ISLAND

"The enemy continued to pour shot and shell into Fort Bartow, which, in less than two hours, became a total ruin."

War Pictures The Fall of Roanoke

Interior of Fort Bartow

The handful of Confederate troops attempting to prevent the Union soldiers from coming ashore at Ashby's Landing were forced to retreat to a three-gun earthwork at the center of the island. Any other outcome would have been a miracle, considering that Confederate Colonel Shaw had only 2,500 men under his command to defend the entire island, versus at least 12,000 Union troops.

Not only were the Confederate forts poorly situated, but the three-gun earthwork, where most of the fighting occurred, was virtually indefensible. The engineers who had designed the plan erroneously believed that the marshes and swamps on either side were impassable. The Confederate forces that had retreated to this spot soon found themselves the focus of an all-out Federal assault.

Ashby's Landing, Roanoke Island

Three-gun earthwork with 32 lb. Barbette Guns

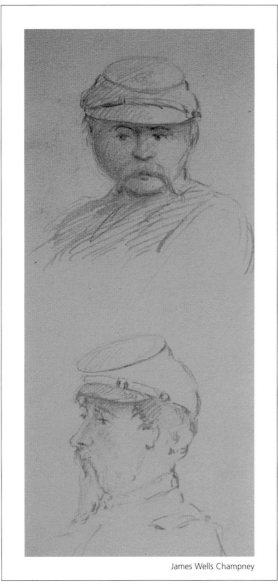

We were up to our knees in mud and water, so their shot passed over us without doing much damage… We could stand on a bog and cut away the briars in front of us and jump to another one; where they were not too large we could crawl through them, tearing not only our clothes but our hides as well.[8]

Shortly after the Union forces came ashore, the rain began to fall relentlessly. The rain-soaked soldiers stood by fires until morning at which point they then began to advance toward the three-gun battery. A soldier in the 25th Massachusetts Volunteer described it this way:

James Wells Champney

This sketch shows the character in the soldier's faces.

Landing area of troops

THE CIVIL WAR ON ROANOKE ISLAND

left: Landing area of Federal troops

Roanoke Island

More than 4,000 Union soldiers came ashore so quickly that they were quite confused regarding what type of enemy they were really facing and what plan of action they were to follow. The muddy, chilly, and rainy conditions only added to the problem. Charles F. Johnson of *Hawkins Zouaves* described his predicament as follows:

> In landing I was separated from my company and had to make my way through the marsh alone. A flimsy, corduroy road of fence-rails had been improvised…I finally got through this and found the bivouac of the troops. They occupied a field of some 20 acres around a farmhouse, which served as General Burnside's *headquarters. Ten thousand men were bivouacked on this field, ranged in huddling groups around hundreds of campfires, and a cold drizzling rain fell almost incessantly during the night.*[9]

Burnside's Headquarters

Burnside's Headquarters

Bivouac

As the Federal troops secured their foothold at Ashby's Harbor, Confederate forces were concentrating their efforts for defense of the island at the three-gun battery near the island's center.

Meanwhile, at Fort Bartow, north of Ashby's Harbor, Confederate troops experienced the devastation wrought by shells from 40 naval guns aimed directly at them. The Federal vessels maintained an uninterrupted fire for more than six hours, withdrawing at dark.

Aerial view of Fort Bartow

The capture of Roanoke Island, February 8, 1862, by the expedition under the command of General Burnside.

Monument to the heroes of the Confederacy in Elizabeth City.

The next morning, the engagement resumed at about 9 a.m. and continued until 12:30, during which several of the men defending Fort Bartow were killed or injured. Private William C. Dawson witnessed the death of the color bearer of the 17th North Carolina Regiment's flag. Dawson ran forward and rescued the colors, and was able to hide the flag in his overcoat's lining until the War's end.

Return fire from some of the 32 pounders at Fort Bartow produced some damage to the *Commodore Perry* and *Hunchback* of the Union fleet.

The actual Confederate flag that flew over Fort Bartow, and kept by William C. Dawson.

Commodore Perry

Present-day photograph of a 32 pdr Barbette gun at Fort Branch, North Carolina, similar to those used on Roanoke Island.

Builders name plate recovered from the *CSS Curlew*

Commodore William F. Lynch attempted to divert attention from Fort Bartow by moving his ships toward the Confederate naval obstructions, but he received too much attention from the Federal naval guns as the *Forrest* and *Curlew* were hit and removed from action. The Federal naval bombardment was so intense that the Confederates eventually evacuated Fort Bartow.

Commodore Perry

Fort Bartow

THE CIVIL WAR ON ROANOKE ISLAND

CSS Curlew under Federal Navy gunfire

USS Hunchback gun crew

Present-day obstructions in Croatan Sound off Roanoke Island.

The tugboat *Tempest* getting the gunboat *Ranger* off a bank, and towing her out of the fire of Fort Bartow.

Blowing up obstructions in Croatan Sound

Obstructions placed by the Confederates in Croatan Sound—Sunken vessels and Chevaux De Frise

Landing of National troop's on Roanoke Island, under cover of Union gunboats *Delaware* and *Picket*

Crew of the *USS Hunchback*

Officers of the *USS Hunchback*

Federal fleet in Croatan Sound

"The troops began to land about 4 p.m. in Ashby's Harbor, on the north side, in front of Hartman's house…each steamer towing boats filled with men, landed in about 20 minutes over 4,000 men." —William L. Welch

THE CIVIL WAR ON ROANOKE ISLAND

Aerial of Elizabeth City Harbor

Commodore Lynch met with the vessels' captains, and the group determined that, in an attempt to save the fleet, they would sail to Elizabeth City on the Pasquotank River. Lynch hoped to obtain ammunition supplies from Norfolk carried through the Dismal Swamp Canal, although this left Colonel Shaw and the Confederates under him without the naval support of the *Mosquito Fleet* and any effective means of leaving Roanoke Island.

The *Mosquito Fleet* sailed north the night of February 7th through the Albemarle Sound toward Elizabeth City with all lights extinguished in order to avoid detection by the Federal fleet. Lieutenant Parker described the scene:

> *It was one of the darkest nights I ever knew, and as none of the vessels showed a light it was difficult to avoid a collision.*[10]

Albemarle Sound

THE CIVIL WAR ON ROANOKE ISLAND

skirmishers to the right of the earthwork, while the 46th Virginia, under Captain Wise (son of General Wise), were deployed as skirmishers to the left.

These skirmishers on either side of the three-gun battery never expected to see Federal soldiers flanking them from both sides of the swamp, because Confederate engineers had declared these heavily-wooded marshes impassable. In addition, the Confederates at Supple's Hill had cut all trees up to a half-mile wide and four hundred yards long in front of the three-gun battery. This provided an unobstructed view of the enemy's approach. They also left all the boughs on the trees, making it difficult for the Federals to maintain a constant line of fire and climb over the boughs at the same time.

Colonel Charles Russell

Back at the three-gun battery near the center of the island, known as Supple's Hill, Confederate forces were under the command of William B. Selden. The infantry supporting this battery consisted of about 500 men from several companies of the 8th North Carolina, two companies of the 31st North Carolina, and two companies of the 46th and 59th Virginia Regiments. Captain Cole and Rangers of the 59th Virginia were deployed as

Major General John G. Foster

Welch of the 23rd Massachusetts described what he experienced:

We marched along about a mile or so from Ashby's Harbor when we heard firing. Soon we came to a clearing and saw the 25th in action ahead of us, with skirmishers ahead. We fell into column by division behind them, advanced when they did, and halted when they did. We were just in range of the bullets and their song was quite audible.[11]

General Foster, with the 25th Massachusetts, 10th Connecticut, and 9th New York, attempted a frontal assault, but experienced heavy casualties. For many of these soldiers, this was their first exposure to enemy fire, so the advance was eventually halted. Private

Ships making their way toward the Roanoke Island Marshes Lighthouse.

Calm Before The Storm

Union General Reno began a flanking movement to the enemy's right with soldiers of the 51st New York, 21st Massachusetts, 9th New York, and the 51st Pennsylvania. The 23rd Massachusetts, 27th Massachusetts, and 4th Rhode Island flanked from the enemy's left. Again, Private Welch described how difficult it was to advance:

> We were ordered by the right flank across the fire of guns, into the woods and swamp to try and flank the enemy. We…passed through the woods…came to an open morass, and skirted the woods to our left, keeping close to them, made as fast as we could for the enemy. We were seen as soon as we emerged, and were fired on, but kept going. We were some three hours getting through this swamp.[12]

Parke's soldiers, aware that the right side of the earthwork had been successfully flanked, ordered men of the 9th New York, led by Rush Hawkins, to charge.

Inside the Confederate earthwork, Lieutenant William B. Selden continued to put up a fight. His brave struggle was described in the following way…

This flanking movement continued on both sides. The soldiers worked their way through the swamps and cut away with swords at the thick vines and brambles. By the time they advanced to the three-gun battery, it had already been overrun by some of Reno's men. At this point, Union General

1862 Non-Commissioned Officers sword, Union

This is similar to a 32 pound Barbette gun used at a three-gun earthwork on Roanoke Island.

sighting, stepped back, and was actually making the motion to jerk the lanyard, when a bullet from the rifle of a Union soldier…pierced his brain, and he fell forward across his gun.[13]

Confederate soldier marker

…young Selden still worked his gun, which bore directly on the advancing regiment…Deliberately lowering his piece and reloading, he seized the lanyard in his own hand and attempted to fire. The primer failed. Cooly securing and adjusting a new primer, he once more sighted and screwed down his gun so that it would rake mercilessly through the ranks now close upon him. He straightened himself from the

Charge of Colonel Rush Hawkins and the 9th New York Zouaves.

Shoulder boards from Captain Wise's uniform.

As the Federals continued their flanking movements, their casualties increased. The soldiers, advancing toward the three-gun earthwork, passed the wounded and dead along the way. Charles F. Johnson of the 9th New York expressed his reaction to entering actual combat for the first time:

I remember that a sort of sickening sensation as if I was going to a slaughter-house to be butchered…I was simply walking into the jaws of death for the first time, made more horrible by the sights and sounds around me, and I felt I must be deathly pale. [14]

In addition to adjusting to the ghastly horrors of battle, some Federal soldiers struggled to overcome complete confusion as they found themselves firing at their own troops on either side of the swamp. At about this time, the command to "charge" was given to *Hawkins Zouaves* and they advanced rapidly on their quest to overrun the three-gun earthwork at Supple's Hill. The Confederate troops who remained at this site were surrounded on each side, so they fled to the rear to avoid capture or death. Before they retreated, Confederate Captain O. Jennings Wise of the 46th

Virginia (Richmond Blues) put up a last-ditch effort to resist. He ordered his men to fire from behind trees, while he moved openly among his men, encouraging them to hold their ground. In doing this, he left himself fully exposed to the concentrated fire of two Federal regiments, and was shot through the wrist with a mini-ball, and later wounded from additional fire. Eventually, Wise was carried to a nearby farmhouse, where he received medical attention from Federal physicians in vain—it was too late.

Federal Medical Corp caps

Confederates defending their position at Supples Hill.

Capture of Roanoke Island, *Charge of the Zouaves*

THE CIVIL WAR ON ROANOKE ISLAND

Colonel Rush Hawkins and men

Hawkins Zouaves charge of Supples Hill.

THE CIVIL WAR ON ROANOKE ISLAND

Edwin Graves Champney

Lieutenant Colonel Victor DeMonteuil

Charles F. Johnson

THE CIVIL WAR ON ROANOKE ISLAND

Black Union soldiers monument in Hertford, North Carolina, est. 1758

Once members of the 25th Massachusetts and 9th New York overran the three-gun battery at Supple's Hill, the Confederates fled toward the north end of the island, with the Federals fast on their heels. A soldier in the 51st Pennsylvania Volunteers described it this way:

So close was the race that the fleeing "Johnnies" had strewn the roadside for miles with everything that was the least cumbersome to them in their precipitate flight....

Take Care

Charge of the 9th New York

THE CIVIL WAR ON ROANOKE ISLAND

THE CIVIL WAR ON ROANOKE ISLAND

Weapons collection of Alex Leary

…Haversacks, canteens, knapsacks, blankets, clothing of all kinds, swords, bowie knives, pistols, cartridge boxes, muskets, belts, and rations, literally covered the ground for six miles. So anxious were they to escape the invaders that they shot their mules and horses, leaving them to die in the road,

rather than let them fall alive into the hands of the "Cused Yankees."[15]

The Confederates fled to the north end of the island in a futile effort to escape capture. However, with the *Mosquito Fleet* gone, there was no alternative but to surrender. At about 3:30 p.m. on February 8th, the Confederates

surrendered unconditionally to Union forces, and shortly thereafter, Confederate reinforcements arrived. Men of the 46th Virginia and the 2nd North Carolina came ashore from a Confederate gunboat, just in time to become prisoners of war. All of the Federal troops began to sweep the island to identify and take control of the Confederate barracks and fortifications.

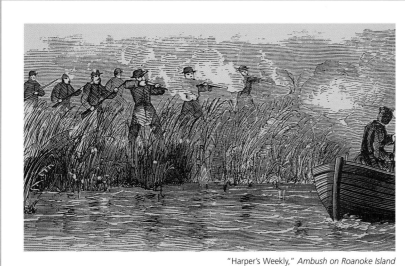

"Harper's Weekly," *Ambush on Roanoke Island*

"Harper's Weekly," *Ambush on Roanoke Island*

Civil War monument on Hatteras Village.

Time to Rest

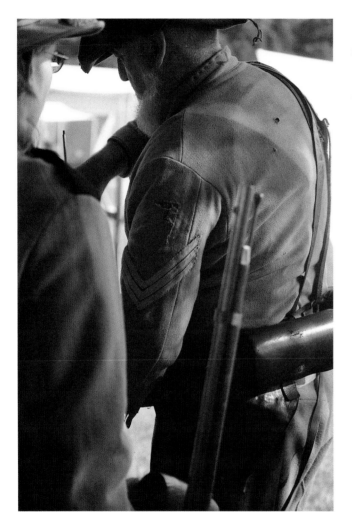

Many of the Union soldiers expressed surprise at the poor quality of weapons and uniforms belonging to their Confederate prisoners:

> The prisoners were a motley looking set, all clothed in a dirty looking homespun gray cloth.... The Wise legion are a more soldierly looking set; they wear gray cloth capes of the same pattern and long sheep's gray overcoats with capes. Most of the officers are smart, good looking young men, wearing well fitting gray uniforms, not unlike those of our own officers.[16]

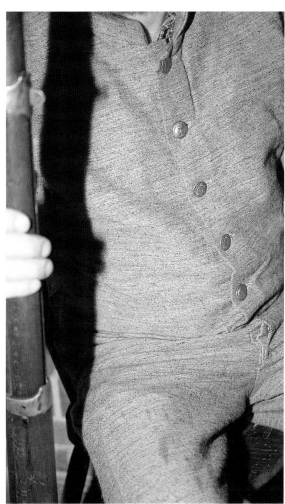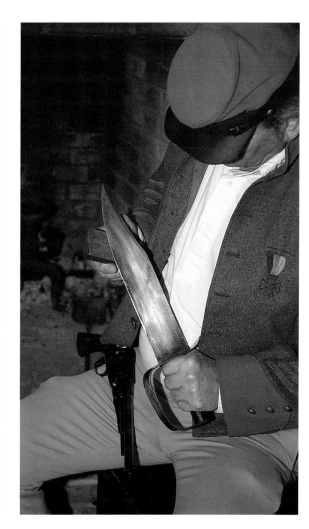

Jarvis Farmhouse

As the Federal troops pursued the retreating Confederates, several of the soldiers from the 9th New York (Hawkins Zouaves) entered the front yard of a farmhouse, which displayed a yellow flag, indicating that it served as a Confederate hospital. Captain Wise was carried to this building, the Jarvis family farmhouse, where he later died.

Like so many houses in the Outer Banks area during this period, the Jarvis home was unpainted, and spots of green moss covered its exterior....

Jarvis House today

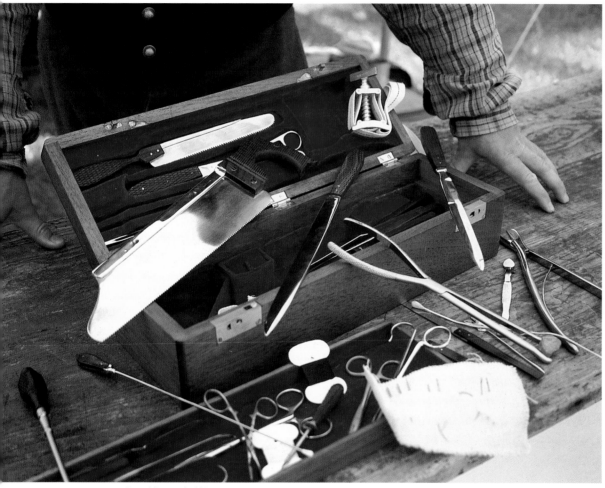

Union soldiers medical kit

Fort Barton Roanoke Island
Sunday Feb 9 1862 8 PM

My dear Father

Thank God my life is spared
and the Stars and Stripes
wave in triumph on Roanoke
Island. We have captured 4 forts, 2 inland
batteries, and taken over 3000 prisoners....

...We lost none. The 8th Conn and 25th Mass suffered considerably. The Spaulding and 2 other steamers leave here tomorrow with the prisoners. Burnsides intends leaving here tomorrow or next day for somewhere. Some Regts will be left here. I will write you particulars in my next. Capt Jennings Wise, son of Gov Wise, was wounded and died last night. He was attended by Surgeon Rivers Love to all good night. I now will turn in not having had much sleep for the past 60 hours for many reasons.

    Affec Your Son

    Wm

Federal Commissioned surgeon with assistants

Confederate prisoners, Roanoke Island

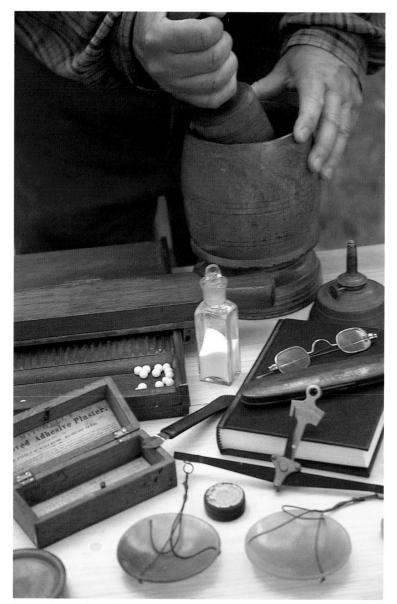

Items used in preparing medicine.

These barracks at Fort Branch in North Carolina depict what life was probably like for the soldiers on Roanoke Island.

made huge fires and stripping off their clothes, wrung out the water and dried them by the fires; then sank down on the floors of their quarters…all were soon asleep."[17]

Nearby, the Confederates had erected barracks for a great many soldiers, which varied in size and quality of construction, although the best quality was obviously reserved for the officers' use. Union soldiers immediately took control and occupancy of these upscale barracks, where they could finally take shelter from the rain and cold, and clean themselves and their mud-soaked clothes.

A number of the 51st Pennsylvania Volunteers said, "After being assigned to quarters in the late rebel barracks, the men

This paper I "captured" in Fort Bartow the afternoon we took possession of it

1862
Camp Park Roanoke Island Feb 25
12:30 PM

My dear Father

My heart felt light to day, for the Chaplain arrived yesterday with his large mail which received a hearty welcome. Well Father to tell you the truth, now 'tis over. I came near thinking 2 or 3 times that the Burnside Expedition was a failure, I told me so often, but I would not admit it, for I don't believe giving up until the last. My lump of hope is quite large you know!

I notice by the Journal that the 4th & 5th R.I. Regts were left at Hatteras which is a great error. Battery F Capt Belger was left there as they could not be used on the Island. The 5th Battalion was held in reserve we passed them drawn up in the woods on our way to the battle. We crossed an opening about 6000 feet from their battery, Fort Defiance, and took to the swamp in order to get on their left flank. Before we could get through the 9th Hawkins Zouaves, (Col Hawkins is young Nick Browns brother in law, remember me to Nick if you please), Mass 21st charged upon and took the battery. As we came out of he swamp the first thing that caught my eye was the Stars & Stripes waving over Fort Defiance. Father, 'twas a glorious sight I can assure you and I cried for joy as our company crossed the opening in front of the Fort. A solid shot passed to my rear and just over the mens heads and made a crashing among the trees as you can imagine, and bullets flew as thick as mosquitoes in August, but God be praised not one of us was killed or even wounded. Lt Baker and 2 or 3 of the men received each a bullet in their blankets. While in the swamp quite a number of bullets passed over our heads sounding thus yip, yip, yip, and came so near Buck who was standing on a stump that he concluded to reduce his height some foot or two. My men were very eager to fire back but I would not allow it as I was afraid we should kill our own men.

Oh, such a two hours as I passed in that swamp I never want to pass again and such a swamp 'twas

Captain William Chace's letters

a pond filled with little spots of earth. In some places the water was knee deep, sometimes up to the waist, and in many instances over our head and as we came out of the swamp we had to wade through a 30 foot pond up to our waist. We kept right on down the road by the Fort some 2 miles and had just built our camp-fires as we expected to bivouac there that night. "Birney" rode up with his staff and started us off immediately for Fort Bartow also with the Conn 8th. We threw out skirmishes with Companies D & I when within a mile of the Fort, as we expected to find a force of 1000 men, we were happily disappointed and when marching into the Fort found it entirely deserted. The guns, 9 in all, 8 smooth 32 pounders and 1 rifled gun throwing an 80 lb shell. We immediately lashed our silk regimental Stars and Stripes to their staff which had been shot down and then raised it towards heaven and once more the tears came - I couldn't help it - as I saw that dear old flag, the emblem of liberty, waving in triumph and conquest over a fort erected by or under the direction of, the foulest traitors that ever trod Gods foot stool. And then to hear the cheers of 750 men for the flag, for Burnsides, for our Genl Park, for Col Rodman, for Gen Sprague, and for Rhode Island. Oh would that you all could have been there.

A rebel Regiment was coming down the beach to retake possession of the Fort when seeing our flag they took to the woods and were all bagged by Genl Reno. We bivouacked two nights near the Fort, went aboard the Queen, left her Tuesday Feb 18, and pitched our tents near the beach of Croatan Sound. It is a beautiful camp, a fine pine grove in our rear and a few trees on either side. I think we will stay here some weeks. It is said to be healthy here, the water is quite good, and the Regt is in good health.

What glorious news from Kentucky and Tennessee, I think we can safely say the back-bone of the rebellion is broken. The inhabitants of the Island are Union; in the vote for separation it stood 2 for, to 58 against. We have a contraband for a servant, his name is George Washington Chace and he is a perfect specimen of a full blooded negro, it matters not what he's doing let the band play and he goes to dancing. He is the life of the camp. If he chances to be going by any of the Company quarters some of the men will sing out, "Come George, give us a song." I am going to bring him home with me.

And now dear Father good bye, and let us all pray that the time is near at hand when that 1,200,000 now in arms may be all returned to their homes and strive in ways that are honorable and noble to support our flag which is the emblem of the greatest and most liberal government this world has ever known. Sincere love to all with reverence and affect.

Your Son Wm

In the morning, feeling refreshed, these soldiers roamed the island looking for Confederate prisoners and supplies. They were successful in finding both. In addition to rounding up prisoners, they found large quantities of sweet potatoes, salt fish, and molasses.

A few days after the capture of the island, the Union troops took control of a small grocery store located about 10 miles below the barracks. They seized the contents, despite protests by the proprietor, and sold the inventory to fellow soldiers. One soldier described it this way:

> ...the Fifty-firsters ransacked the while building, and finally found a whole barrel of hams covered over with trash. He soon supplied the applicants with these hams, at 10¢ per pound...In hunting the hams, he had found whiskey and filled the canteens at $2 each.[18]

These Union soldiers harassed the store owner until he reluctantly abandoned all efforts to retake possession of his own store.

Union soldiers and Confederate prisoners socializing on Roanoke Island.

Over 3000 prisoners
140 commis officers

Steamer E Queen
Off Fort Barlow
Tuesday Feb 11 9 AM

My dear Father

All well, all our Regt "present or accounted for." A lovely morning for us to start on our trip somewhere across Albemarle Sound. Our men are in high spirits, our victory is complete. Our gunboats went after the rebel fleet night before last and have not been heard from since, so I think they must have accomplished something. Get the New York news for then you might find a correct account as the reporter was on the ground for I saw him. Good morning all.
Affec
Wm S Chace

Roanoke Island Marshes

Commander C.S. Rowan

The Mosquito Fleet Destroyed at Elizabeth City

*M*eanwhile, Confederate Commodore Lynch was unable to sail north on Albemarle Sound without being detected by the Union forces during the evening of February 7th. The *Seabird* led the way, towing the *Forrest* with the *Black Warrior, Raleigh,* *Beaufort, Ellis,* and *Fanny* following. Their movement up the Sound was discovered by the Federal fleet under the command of Commander C.S. Rowan. In his official report dated February 11, 1862, Rowan wrote the following:

> As the (Confederate) flotilla passed into the sound the smoke of two rebel steamers was reported close in toward the opposite shore, these steamers apparently heading for the Pasquotank River. I made signal to chase, and steered to cut off the enemy, but he succeeded in entering the river, and, as night was closing on us, I ordered the chase to discontinue.[19]

Federal pursuit continued throughout the morning, with 14 Union gunboats traveling the Pasquotank River. They discovered Commodore Lynch's *Mosquito Fleet* drawn up behind a four-gun battery (fort) at Cobb's Point. The odds were overwhelmingly in favor of the Federal fleet, as they had 32 guns and 14 vessels, versus 8 guns and 6 ships on the Confederate side. Lynch ordered Captain Parker and men from his crew on the *Beaufort* to man the guns at the fort and fire on the enemy. A pilot was assigned to take the *Beaufort* on toward Norfolk.

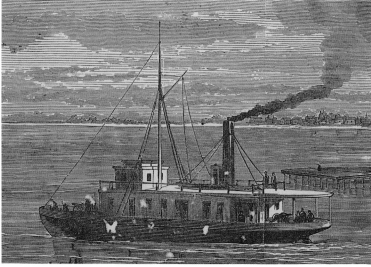

Fanny

Aerial view of Cobb's Point

passed by the flotilla and attack it in reverse.[20]

Vessels on both sides of the battle were low on ammunition, and Commander Rowan ordered his men not to fire until they were within sure range of the Fort and Lynch's fleet. The Confederate line of defense was drawn diagonally across the river in front of the town.

The Confederates opened fire first, both from the Fort at Cobb's Point and the *Black Warrior*.

On board the Federal vessel *Delaware*, Commander Rowan ordered all of his ships into the following formation:

The Underwriter, Perry, Morse, *and* Delaware *in advance to reconnoiter with* the little Ceres *on their right flank, followed by the remainder of the force, led in order by the* Louisiana *and* Hetzel, *the* Valley City, *and* Whitehead *under orders to leave the lines as soon as the battery had been*

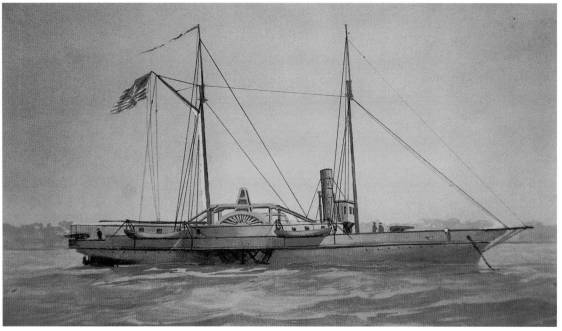
USS Hetzel

The Union fleet's guns remained silent as they continued their advance among the shot and shell falling thick and fast around them. Commander Rowan reported, "When within three-quarters of a mile of the battery I made signal, 'Dash at the enemy'. Our fire was then opened with telling effect, and our vessels put to utmost speed."[21]

The unfaltering advance of the Union vessels demoralized and humiliated the Confederates. The *Black Warrior* was set on fire and abandoned by her officers and crew. Lieutenant Flusser of the *Perry* rammed and sank the *Seabird*, taking her officers and crew prisoner. The *Ceres* captured the *Ellis*. Confederate midshipman William C. Jackson was wounded by musketry as he attempted to swim away from the *Ellis*, and was then taken aboard the *Hetzel*, where he died from his wounds. He was later taken ashore and buried in the Fort. The *Forrest* was burned by Confederates as she lay on the ways at the shipyard in Elizabeth City, while the *Delaware* pursued and captured the *Fanny*.

Three or four of the Federal vessels sailed up the river to the wharves and waterfront of Elizabeth City, but the Confederates attempted to torch the city rather than allow it to fall into Union hands. Commander Rowan reported the following:

A battery of field artillery was seen making a hasty retreat down the street. A party of our people passing through the streets came suddenly upon a mounted artillery officers of the Wise Legion, who, in obedience to orders from General Henningsen, was compelling the defenseless people to set fire to the houses. Several houses were set on fire before he was arrested and brought to me. …No other houses were destroyed besides those set on fire under the direction of Lieutenant Scruggs, of the Wise Legion.[22]

River view past…

…and present

S.E. Queen Feb 11 1862
12:30 PM

Dear Father
    The Commodore of
our fleet has just come
down from the site of
Elizabeth City.
The fleet took the
battery just below the
city. The city was fired
by the rebels, three of their gunboats are taken, one gunboat - a NY ferry
boat - ran into a rebel gunboat and nearly cut her in two, then boarded
her and whipped them
with clubs. Burnside's
"uncertain" Expedition
thus far has proved
quite successful in my
humble opinion.

        Affec Your Son
        Wm Stillwell

P.S. We are now getting
underway for somewhere

Mosquito Fleet being hit by Union fire.

Actual cannon carriage recovered from the *Black Warrior* located in Albemarle Sound off Cobb's Point.

Destruction of the Mosquito Fleet at the battle of Elizabeth City, 1862

that their houses be spared, and they were. What had been the commissary store house, however, was seized, and the Union officers took fresh supplies of beef, bread, and flour. Quickly and quietly, Elizabeth City fell under Federal control.

Some Elizabeth City citizens came to the waterfront to ask

Grice-Fearing House, circa 1798

Tillet-Nixon House, circa 1860

This house has a typical floorplan from the 1860's with a center hallway and parlors on either side, circa 1885.

Pool-Lumsden-Peters House, Elizabeth City, North Carolina, 1840

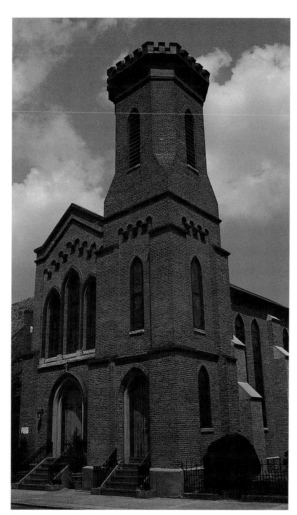

Christ Episcopal Church, circa 1856

Charles-Hussey House, 1849

Back on Roanoke Island, some of the Union troops settled into the barracks, which had been built by the Confederates at Camp Reno (formerly Fort Huger). These Union forces considered themselves fortunate to be housed in buildings rather than sleeping on the ground or in tents. Charles Johnson of the 9th New York said, "Each apartment is provided with a fireplace and chimney, a luxury which we never had since we entered the service of Uncle Sam."[23]

Barracks at Fort Branch, similar to housing used on Roanoke Island.

find anything related to Sir Walter Raleigh's "lost colony:"

This being a warm sunny day, a small party of us thought…we might find some traces or relics of Raleigh's expedition. …Whipple picked up an old shoe heel. Here was a prize, surely a veritable relic of Raleigh's party. …It was pretty warm; the water looked clear and refreshing. Some one proposed taking a dip. No sooner said than

Civil War soldiers' pipes found on Roanoke Island.

off came our clothes and in we plunged. …The water was ice cold, and I thought I should certainly freeze before getting out…[24]

In their spare time, some Union soldiers decided to explore the island. Several amused themselves by carving pipes from briar roots, while others studied the history and culture of Roanoke Island. Private D.L. Day of the 25th Massachusetts described his efforts to

Fort Branch, North Carolina

James Wells Champney

These sketches of barracks at Fort Macon depict what life was probably like for soldiers on Roanoke Island.

Union soldiers and Confederate soldiers socializing at a prison camp on Roanoke Island.

James Wells Champney

A soldier relaxing and writing home, as one may have done after the capture on Roanoke Island.

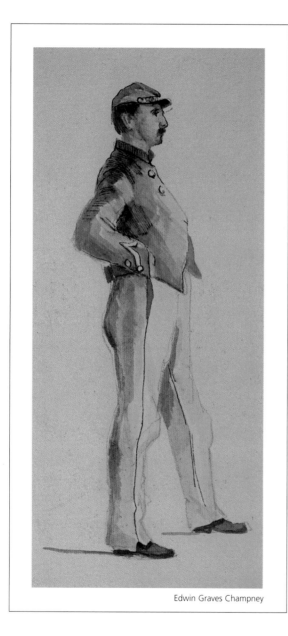

Edwin Graves Champney

Many Union soldiers socialized with the prisoners, and exchanged buttons, jack knives and other small items. Confederate officers were later paroled and sent to Elizabeth City, where an exchange of prisoners took place.

Most of the Union soldiers were surprised to discover how swampy and small

ELIZABETH CITY, N.C.

"On Sunday, the 16th, General Burnside came aboard and announced that we could all be released on a parole of honor. But it was not until the next Thursday that they moved with us, then steamers, bearing all the prisoners taken, started for Elizabeth City, where, on Friday, we landed and were released."

E.R. Liles
The Fall of Roanoke Island
North Carolina Troops, 1861-65

Exchange of Confederate prisoners, Elizabeth City, North Carolina.

Roanoke Island was. One of the soldiers said, "The island is about 10 or 12 miles long, and from 1 to 3 miles wide, lying nearly level with the waters of the sounds."[25] They also discovered that most of the local residents sold fish and, up to the time of the war, traded with the North. Horses looked extremely small and wore no collars when pulling a cart or wagon. The same soldier said the following:

> ...the hames, resting on the bare shoulder, and a rope or bridle compose all the harness needed or used. The cows are very small, none of which weigh over 200 or 250 pounds, and are very poor. The farmers raise Indian corn and sweet potatoes, but nothing else. The land is worth from $2.50 to $3.00 per acre; choice tracts $5.00 per acre. The frogs are croaking and the crickets chirping every night...[26]

Monument in Hertford, North Carolina (est. 1758) dedicated to the black soldiers who served for the Union during the Civil War.

Establishment of the Freedmen's Colony

As with Hatteras Island, it did not take long for word to reach the slaves on the mainland that Roanoke Island was now controlled by Union forces. Soon, large numbers of slaves began

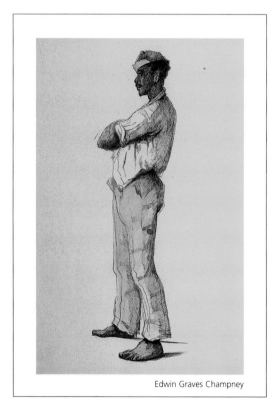

Edwin Graves Champney

arriving, where they were considered "contraband" and declared free. Numbers of new arrivals increased to such an extent that Federal forces did not know how to cope with sanitation, housing, and other problems. General Foster appointed Reverend Horace James, an Army Chaplain from Massachusetts, to supervise the establishment of a colony for these runaway slaves. The black men were seen as possible recruits for the Union Army, and a large tract of land was appropriated for the refugee families.

Almost immediately, northern states organized a National Freedman's Relief Association in February 1862. They appealed to the wealthy and well-to-do to provide aid, and set about to appoint "teachers to instruct the Freedmen in industrial and mechanical arts, in the rudiments of education, the principles of Christianity, their accountability to the laws of God and man, their relationship to each other as social beings, and all that might render them competent to sustain themselves as members of a civilized society."[27]

Most of the teachers who arrived on the island to educate the former slaves were missionaries. In addition to religious instruction, an industrial school operated from November 25, 1865 through July 27, 1866.

As the war neared its end, many of the black men serving in the Union Army came back to the island, at which point, both governmental and private support for the colony declined. Sadly, the freed slaves received a huge setback when the land that had been given to them was taken away and returned to its original owners. Eventually, many of the families were forced to move away in order to find work, although some struggled to the very end to hold on to their land.

Shackles of former slaves found on Roanoke Island.

Meanwhile, the Federal Army on Roanoke Island boarded the transport vessels that had once carried them to Roanoke Island. They left three regiments to occupy the island: the 9th New York, the 89th New York, and the 6th New Hampshire. The rest sailed from Roanoke Island on the 11th of March 1862, to sail to Hatteras and then on to Newbern, North Carolina. General Burnside was aware of the strategic importance of capturing Newbern: if the Federals captured this city on the mainland, they could then threaten Confederate supply lines and bring more of eastern North Carolina and its inland waters under the control of the Union. Eventually, Union troops were engaged in battles at Newbern, Beaufort, Phymouth, South Mills, and Wilmington and other communities of eastern North Carolina.

James Wells Champney

"Our expedition moves in a day or two for somewhere and...

...I trust the same good fortune may attend us here."

....Peace & Freedom Forever

Original Photo Credits

Beverly R. Robinson Collection, USNA Museum, Annapolis, MD, front cover, pp. 66, 67, 87

The Chrysler Museum of Art, p.2

Peter Rascoe, p. 69 (flag)

North Carolina Department of Cultural Resources/Underwater Archaeology, pp. 70 (plate), 122 (gun carriage)

"I notice the R I 4th is not mentioned by any of the papers, well we were there. Love to all, Good Night Love to family & friends."

Affec Your Brother Wm

Bibliography

Barrett, John G. (1963) *The Civil War In North Carolina.* Chapel Hill: University of North Carolina Press.

Bobyshell, Oliver C. (1895) *The 48th In the War: Being a Narrative of the Campaigns of the 48th Regiment, Infantry, Pennsylvania Veteran Volunteers, During the War of the Rebellion.* Philadelphia: Avil Printing.

Day, D.L. (1883) *My Diary of Rambles with the 25th Mass. Volunteer Infantry, with Burnside's Coast Division, 18th Army Corps and Army of the James,* Milford: King and Billings.

Edmonds, Thomas F. (1885) *Operations On the Atlantic Coast, II Operation In North Carolina 1861-1862, 24th Massachusetts Volunteers.* Papers of the Military Historical Society of Massachusetts.

Gould, Joseph (1908) *The Story of the Forty Eighth.* Record of the Forty Eighth Regiment Pennsylvania Volunteer Infantry, Mt. Carmel, PA.

Hawkins, Rush C. (1996) *The War of the Rebellion: A compilation of the Official Records of the Union and Confederate Armies,* Ser. I, Vol. IV. In the Civil War CD-ROM. Developed by Phillip Oliver. Carmel, IN: Guild Press of Indiana.

Hill, D.H., Jr. *Confederate Military History,* The Blue and Gray Press, Vol. IV.

Johnson, Charles F. (1986) *The Long Roll: Impressions of a Civil War Soldier.* Reprint of 1911 edition, Carabelle, Shepherdstown.

Mallison, Fred M. (1998) *The Civil War On the Outer Banks: A History of the Late Rebellion Along the Coast of North Carolina from Carteret to Currituck.* McFarland, Jefferson.

Parker, William H. *Recollections of a Naval Officer,* Naval Institute Press, Edited by Craig L. Symonds.

Rhode Island Soldiers and Sailors Historical Society (1880) *Personal Narratives of Events In the War of the Rebellion,* Providence: N. Bangs Williams & Co.

Scharf, Thomas J. (1996) *History of the Confederate State Navy,* New York: Gramercy Books.

Trotter, William R. (1989) *Ironclads and Columbiads: The Civil War in North Carolina.* Winston-Salem: John Blair.

Endnotes

1　Private Osborne, Battle of Roanoke Island, p.50.

2　My Diary Rambles with the 25th Massachusetts, p.35.

3　The Long Roll, p. 89.

4　Recollections of a Naval Officer, pp. 226–247.

5　Private Osborne, Massachusetts 23rd Volunteers, pp. 53–54.

6　Soldiers & Sailors, p. 31.

7　Recollections of a Naval Officer, p. 248.

8　My Diary Rambles with the 25th Massachusetts Volunteer Infantry, p. 35

9　The Long Roll, pp. 90–91.

10　Recollection of a Naval Officer, p. 25.

11　Private Osborne, Massachusetts 23rd Volunteers, p. 56.

12　Private Osborne, Massachusetts 23rd Volunteers, p. 56.

13　The End of An Era, The Roanoke Island Tragedy, p. 187.

14　The Long Roll, p. 93.

15　History of the 51st Regiment of Pennsylvania Volunteers, p. 78.

16　My Diary of Rambles with the 25th Massachusetts Volunteer Infantry, pp. 37–38.

17　History of the 51st Regiment of Pennsylvania Volunteers, p. 83.

18　History of the 51st Regiment of Pennsylvania Volunteers, p. 84.

19　Official Records of the Navies, Report of Commander Rowan Series I, Vol. 6, pp. 546–611.

20　Official Records of the Navies, Report of Commander C.S. Rowan, pp. 546–611.

21　Official Records of the Navies, Report of C.S. Rowan, pp. 546–611.

22　Official Records of the Navies, Report of Commander Rowan, pp. 546-611.

23　The Long Roll, p. 108.

24　My Diary of Rambles with the 25th Massachusetts Volunteer Infantry, pp. 38–40.

25　History of the 51st Regiment, Pennsylvania Volunteers, p. 88.

26　History of the 51st Pennsylvania Regiment, p. 88.

27　"First Annual Report of the National Freedmen's Relief Association," New York, February 19th, 1863.